Mermaid's Purse

Laynie Browne

SPUYTEN DUYVIL

New York City

Grateful acknowledgement to the editors of the following journals in which some of
these poems have appeared:
*Common Knowledge, Conjunctions: The Web Forum of Innovative Writing, Fourteen
Hills, Fragments, Inscape, Object + Torque collaborative issue, non,
Rhizome,* and *The Washington Post.*
Poems from this manuscript also appeared in the following anthologies:
Poet's Choice edited by Robert Hass, Knopf 1998.
Writing on Water edited by David Rothenberg & Marta Ulvaeus, Terra Nova 2001.
Thanks to Chris Funkhouser.
The Poet's Calendar edited by Douglas Messerli, Sun & Moon.

Many thanks to Susan Sanford for her careful reading of the final text.
Special thanks to Brad Davidson, also to the University of Washington's Friday Harbor
Laboratories, where much of this work was written.

for Brad

"Because my memory is undergoing a sea-change. Though I am certain I remember, I am no longer sure what it is I remember nor, indeed, the reason I should remember it"

—*Angela Carter*

A "mermaid's purse"
is the discarded egg casing of a sea skate

1

Eyes open among a berth of shadows. I saw a circle composed of my arrival and another's departure. All of my thoughts wash away like ghosts running towards a ship which I did not recognize. I cannot lend you a copy of my voyage, as all passages have grown heavy. My guard geese will not always obey. The darkness is unwieldy, but the toss of waters is the same. In a dream he retold his dream, so that he might remember it upon waking. Manatee were once mistaken for mermaids, "sirenius," and so their history was rewritten, flesh, bone, and hide. These lapses where I am unable to say anything in response to a bracelet of ice.

2

Enamel perchance toils, in a many tiered sea-flower. A palette torn by sand. The hour is a matter to leave upon a doorstep. A blue empire. There is furniture which cannot be carried. Bones against faint white skies. As one who attempts to live among the ruinous mirrors of ocean carries an oxygen tank without end. I turn on my head to imagine the way clocks flow backwards. And water is taken up into the sky.

3

Influence is the type of soft cloth I wrap around my shoulders unknowingly. It is so easy to open eyes in the pink light of sunrise. I think I'll take a sea voyage, but pick up a book instead. Or as I am drifting I will say Queequeg, three times like a potion, and be off with my light. I remember this sense of water while working on a new device which will allow me to move in relation to the flight of a clock. I sent everything I could think of through the mail. There must be certain days when one is not required to wear shoes or coats or even to speak at all. The pictures on the walls beg my pardon. As the staircase which keeps descending into memory.

4

When she closes her eyes she is but some other water-
mark. All of my sisters live in different cities and mark
time by the colors of changing dresses. I see them now
arriving in droves for a visit. The black cat maiden
begins her ascent to the upper worlds, carrying with her
a small candle. When the face of the clock is nearby, I
cannot deny anything to those who beg according to the
hour, and even stand on the table at times. But all of that
is now under our skirts. We find our means of winter
heat. A ginger bath, or a brew of three kinds of flowers.
Plants marry in secret, those ferns and mosses.

5

Rolled backwards upon a lost vehicle, a rectangular parting with time. When the ground beneath me had stopped changing, I awoke to find a similar pattern in my hands. If I were not to endeavor to move those sightless forms, I would lie nowhere, my bed no longer earth. Whose words around my neck, that charm. As the sky has countless times conspired upon a low level to lift my eyes. The light puckers. I respond accordingly, moving uphill. The gradual decline of days is the unstrung purse left lying upon a forgotten bench. My place has been accorded by nightfall.

6

The distance between my lives is perplexing. Singed paper cheeks and lashes. My dwellings have passed into unknown guardian's faces, taking on the shape of the hemisphere I call ash. The ash children. Only dawn may speak of paper curtains, lips parted. Umbrellas carefully charted the journey. I've ordered my veil. I have no wish to emerge, unwrap my face from tulle, remove the mist garb from fingertips. I have no wish to step away from a teahouse.

7

Those nameless birds followed our thoughts, holding their wings open to dry in the cold. Towing gauze, to wrap and stow, fearful of breakage. I remove this outer frock and this carriage. A false candelabra. It is not I who carry their images away. I woke to find feathers near my head, talons and earth. A fledgling had stolen the banks upon which I slept. The notion that bad luck followed her like a clock is false. The morning is no explanation for what comes before, and vanishes just as easily.

8

A tree translates the double horizon. The day nods, filling pods with blue-gray. The crossbow principle does not apply here. Why do blue flowers yield red dye, and yellow flowers red? They first heard the house calling, and then went walking. Collecting samples from the spirit world. A completely round rainbow. This is the sound of falling asleep suddenly. If I can remember not to do so upon a wheel's edge.

9

If I am powerless to alleviate the distress of others, I am also powerless to shed a garment of malevolence, since it fuses with form. My physical location is indescribable, as my mind is unable to shed impressions of earlier designs. Instead I carry with me every past dwelling, and lay down only the heaviest homes while resting. When I rise, I rinse off my homes of sleep and walk carefully across the page. I find an abode in the voices of others, yet they cannot be assembled, and there is no place where they happen. I desired to carry a trifle of someone else's garment, to afford a companion resolve. My burdens did not outnumber me, but I found it difficult to ask. Even for a cloak sleeve. For any mention of weightiness could cause a trembling, which even my greatest attentions could not ameliorate.

10

In order to turn to February, I must first lift a pattern of disks, emblems upon a branch staff, and a series of pendant reflections. If I sit at dawn, this may coax the sun to wake. The crystalline month has arrived with the deceptive transparencies of early spring. And yet the light has just only begun to return. The sky seems a fragmentary vision. A veil of clouds pulled over the head. A slip cloth for skating the frame of a day. This is how the dawn finds birds. Why mountains follow ice.

11

The course of the spine then is like those dried rushes which go up in flame within the space of an eyelash. It seems a short time before the sky is filled with light. If I sit at dusk, I may quietly lay down bedding. I bring the sun down silently, as anyone would. We recline in order to imitate the horizon. A brick building becomes a cascade of stones. I said goodbye to their piles of coats. At some point in the day I am mastered by silence. I can almost see the crest of passing lacework.

12

Queen's bluff. Three fanning women standing on the edge of a calendar disappeared as molten snow. The winter sun is the bride of this image. I use the night as drawing space, to spread out belongings without care. Projections of faint pillowcases lulled me adrift. I slogged and swam to reach the boat which had already begun, but at the bottom step was told no more boarders would be taken, as a storm was expected. We were absolutely two-dimensional. Like any animal, a boat consumes light. Within the blue night below my window of sea-kale.

13

I seek the secret dwelling places of furl. This is one reason I aspire to emulate plants. Why is it I am unable to speak in sepals? If I linger in gardens where these privileges are possible, there is a season of thought which is permitted to tumble. A corridor uncoils. Bramble may be combed. Coral may be injured by my bare hand. There is a confidential code for navigating such landscapes. If you lean against this branch too quickly, my signs are muffled.

14

As we walked through the arboretum I could speak of
the white watery sky. A winter blossom, both green and
bell-like. She combed the silk tassel blossoms, releasing
their pollen. Her gray glove covered with yellow dust.
They could have been pendants. Falls added to a cascade
of evening curls. The dust mattered as a form of invita-
tion. A gold cloud which hides the impetus of flight. Of
all things airborne, her hand was most luminous.

15

For a salad of sea lettuces he brought home a small cup of ocean water. Once he arrived home, his cup overflowed. He endeavored to sort the ocean of his rooms, placing aside urchins and fish. He laid out the seaweed in boxes, and turned on taps to rinse. All of his belongings had taken afloat, and yet none of them were harmed. The water enhanced the room, the floors, even his books. When he had finished he opened the door and the ocean returned to its larger rooms. The mineral salts encrusting the walls glowed dimly that evening. Only the lettuces remained.

16

The snow is unwarranted. This reminds him of wisteria hanging down the walls of his years of study. The scent is synonymous with longing. If I write my observations in sleep, I leave no footsteps, and yet I continue to fall in steady patterns. Each flurry is an unduplicatable collection of icons. So thus to coil and uncoil is indispensable like the affluent wish I share with a starfish. To remain fastened to a sea-rock. Past, present and future sight are lenses interchanged fluidly. As if each hypothesis were a parasol which slightly changed the light.

17

Agate beach in rain which fell heavily, creating a pattern of opening and closing cavities of sand. The sound guided further out to sea. Hibernation in winter is the same misrepresentation of venture. If I remain indoors I may travel more easily. Speech mirrors silence the way footsteps would otherwise remain submerged. Ambulation is changed by water. I travel away in order to match the hem of waters. I witness the tide's undermarkings, as if reading a series of utterances. An attempt to study the kaleidoscopic languages.

18

I am not transcribing the sunset because the colors do not transfer. Each dawn compiles rosy fingers. We consisted of our voices alone. A monogram of sounds. She followed him with the hope of surfacing his secrets. She separated her rings, and therefore her fingers. All along while listening outside of the body speaking. If I do not pause, I miss certain sounds, and might never have believed their echoes. The space which has elapsed between is laced with a crepuscular netting.

19

February's pink and red arrows may help me succumb to ageless blossoms. Snow falls heavily. Handwriting to hide stars. A black comb thrown from a window became a primeval forest. As we walked up the stairs, icicles clinging to edges. Placed under a winter's looking glass, a sundered-heart can hardly keep warm. Cinders spilt out into a dark hallway. They may only bleed within present time. And this is why we are indistinguishable from ourselves, our motives.

20

Things not rooted in this world are less elusive in that they may follow me off of a map. *The light in windmills naming wrens.* These semblances evaporate as faint mumblings, and then reappear in puddles. I am unable to travel by roads. The women standing on the edge of a calendar are in epiphany since they stand not within a square, but in an unnumbered space. Thus, they need go nowhere on this particular day. I have tried many times to find this unsquared space, but have failed with drowsy feet. I comb a marble island. In red winter with form unfound.

21

Light flows through this winter curtain. A gold morning flung from custody. A sacred lamp once pulled from a shelf, and easily forgotten. The morning was a pale reminder of Monday, whose lips were painted even in sleep. We had come within arms lengths of ourselves within a river whose boundaries were sinking discrepancies. I must no longer lie down amidst tempests when no one is looking. If only the book had stayed beside me these nights I would never have gone astray. The shadows were not ghosts until you reminded me. I covered my eyes with a sleeve of nodding grasses.

22

The empty space within minutes, where we don't actually live, can be transferred to other deserts where every hour is good company. I am all alone here, not even my watch. I wish to play back those evenings when I might have stayed awake longer to remain in your presence. You arrive barefoot on the brink of my sleep. Summoning. And now the sky, as my signature has passed into evening. An invitation flecked with blue petals. A blackbird swept towards the ground from a tree as if it were merely a dark leaf. And so I believed sitting in front of this horizon, that remarkable talents, just as the drowsy sentiments before passing, are the most secret.

23

I noticed my signature had changed, but how it appeared before this lapse, I cannot be reminded, even by the sight of it, since my wrist has an ambient will. Once having radiated, it continues to create its own peripheries. To remember this ghost was once a leaf is to know the rowing parts of speech. The tableau populates its own hysterics. The head might actually collapse into nothingness were it to stop containing thought. The streets disappeared into snow. The light of streetlamps, a sienna pressed against the blocked outlines of the cedar whose branches make a latticework. I'd rather not turn on the light and banish auburn. My easily lost night, and early river sky.

24

She wanted to give me a bunch of heavy white stars to mark my marriage, and where did I want them. What context, a blue whale. As I lie on the floor with sonatas, refusing to answer anyone. Not even to place another log on the fire. It may go out, I considered, as I may well also go. How pleasant that will be. Some talents will do nothing for one's career. My dreams flee, swimming in an ocean which curled back from both sides, unfurling. I hide things where you may find them if you care to look. I make no outline, but simply lie down and follow the course of my body for any meaningful structure.

25

This refuge without which I would be without locution. A little bouquet here. An opal slip against an edgewise. What "should" be done or accomplished throws a shoe out an alley window. The lantern plant lights the path of the falling slipper. The edge of the city is pins and needles. The nights often painted were lovely, and yet what to do with them? Those thoughts which become objects weigh heavily upon my brow. Until I can spell nothing, not even my name.

26

It was never mentioned why the princess was placed upon the top of the glass mountain, or how she might descend. The red mouth of the river gone astray, hair torn asunder; she walks across the heavens slowly, leaving us for the noon. A simple sweep or curve of concentration. At each portal, an ornament was removed, her robes and garments, a girdle of birthstones. The taught tide across dark eyes, as if rhythm were flowers in their motionless sound. It was she who played upon the zither. Plucked with a plectrum. She carried a spyglass, tossed by waves. A rope of seaweed around her waist.

27

Girls wrapped in towel gowns stood on the shore. Threads of destiny were said to be visible, fastening a wrist to an image. These tasks which I set aside cannot remain undone. Where do shoulders bare their own inferences? They are upon me as minstrels draw the blinds of heavy eyes, as trepidation draws a cord around a neck or an arm ties a sash. And that trembling room into which you wake has also a curtained side. I cannot describe why it is that the task never ends, but only that it is beyond the discipline of movement or breath in the sense that it bids me. There is no date to speak of. No appointments are willing to venture.

28

In the interior chambers of the pinkest enamel, where rest is alchemical, night is a shade slipped over the large face of the earth. A gestural form. We must rely singly on our senses, and follow the signs of daily skies in order to belong within the palm of symmetry. I ask nothing but to wander within these lands which never weary. That I may be a susceptible inhabitant, and walk across the boundaries of trellis needles, where the rest of my slumbering being may be encountered and drawn out from private vessels. We are carting our sorrows away. For this reason my sleepingcar is a woodcarving. Surveying the edges of an untouchable future. With allowances of lime.

29

Once knowing the area of land unbound by memory, there is a series of steps which may be learned from the stepmistress. Through these court lessons you may walk unabided, as if a native, within the untouchable future which now treads upon the soles of your feet. Nevermind, that any such steps at all, as long as one foot were to follow the next in a continuous direction, would allow you to cross over a boundary. It is these habits of mind which disallow the sensation of clear land, and open hemispheres. In the deepest simulacrum, a cloak of silence became a cloak of invisibility. Fever was brought on by pantomime rain. A lost tribe follows their yesterdays markings in order to retrace a happening. There is a small hole where air is imprisoned. I am awake by a light not in the sky or made by any hand.

30

I wrote a series of apologies to a landscape. The yellow geums turned to seed clusters. The face of the stream bank crept into shadow. We avoided treading upon the exposed roots of trees. And walked through this transition as if our arms were streamers. Those things which changed became rocklings. Who will remember which days were exchanged for roots? Leaves may carry a message when circling the body. Sash ideogram.

31

In order to tap into that fairly avid mistress of time, she beheld a blight. A sanctuary in which there remained a quiet ember of time. The rooms run into each other, as the light moves assuring its own agility, promising rooms to be the fluid protectors of those crosshatch demi-worlds. If you push aside a well and come towards wishing you may find the mechanism a contraption well worn, and perhaps not properly cared for. To carry one's head above sea level you invent a curious globe, and then walk towards its edges. The wishing mechanism may seem to disappear in certain light, or testimonial weather. Learning a maze well mostly suggests remaining within it. When I might step out of these caverns, they will no longer exist. No line behind me could begin to show where I have been, and territory cannot be held to speak on account of its former inhabitants.

32

Again I ask the oracle in order to be reminded of my simple coordinates. If I stand in this underlined doorway, there is a place where my feet press into wood, and yet this cannot name the figure, or by what rule it may move. In the manner of a cloudburst influence may wane. A lake has risen not to rest upon virtue. Nine in the second place means arms at evening and at night. Molting, the pelt of an animal. The younger daughter is above. Set the calendar in order and make the seasons clear. The bone I leave isn't left.

33

I keep checking my wrist where no time has been placed. She crept inside a pumpkin shell and there she separated the days. The yolks we fed to the dogs, and the whites we stretched and made filmy screens for the backgrounds of watercolors. The difference between thought and movement is a frond. A white pawed omen. Once morning has passed, all things may overcome me, aisles and pillars, strewn objects, a spot of dove gray on the floor. If there will be any summer from these hands, a toad or a walrus walks with the same intent. The dictionary is lying again. Now the sky is white.

34

A white emblem covers her face. When this dream is carried down a corridor, it becomes very light and very small. So much so, that it may have escaped me entirely. It's high white cliffs and green logic. Sound of everglades. Eels early prayer. There was a curtain parted over her eyes. A careless ship. She carried a hidden crossroad towards the wisp of afternoon.

35

The silence was longitudinal, the way water has no color but reflects. The way a nameless radiance is touched simultaneously with all parts of the body, invisibly. How many letters would I write each day in order to send my thoughts? Fire is the quickest of animals. Which direction has January fled? I woke early to worry. Not to say that I wish I had stopped to gather some of the fallen branches of the cherry. And yet to trim a tree in flower is a violation of the laws of beauty. If you respond within a newfound bark.

36

The notion of descent from trees has been almost lost sight of. Her grandchildren were farthings. Smaller than the needle of a compass, and clearly pointed. Even so, prosperity is still linked with the well being of the tree. Weeds have been worshipped. Corn offered to the blind. Snowdrop, fair maid of February, the fruit of the ash. The earliest gods were rock and mountain. And temples formed by shadow.

Marriage caused the first trembling of the earth. From the roots of the silk cotton tree, cypresses and palms. The tree gave birth to everything that lives. The grove beside remembrance. The tree into which every apprentice drove a nail for luck. Remotest adoration. Serenade a flower until dusk. Fire singing birds. Infants fetched from cabbage.

A hollow tree overhanging a pool is a place of unborn oracles. Bury flour in the course trunk of an oak. This brings prosperity, so reads the fortune of doves. Linden twine was tied to guests at feasts to prevent intoxication. A copper kettle later, this rag which is called courage. I summoned myself to curtsey despite the looming thoughts of stray nimble birds. No less a fly caught in amber. Tree parentage. Pelopiadae, descended from plane.

39

Love's still function. A shipwrecked dove. Confused with fact, the sounds of all clocks. She stepped inside the jasmine bush, at typhoon hour. Perhaps girlhood is also a disguise. Selves are caught in function. Cadences which interrupt the moon. The sighing of water. A blind man piercing a pearl.

40

Haunted by the days' endeavor or lack of endeavor, now that I have found my bearings, dates on a calendar take up several partners at once, and dance. We were born in a house of paper. This vineyard of worry, the grafting of silt upon silt. Bodies fallen together like linkages in a long passage, a truck of sleep. Gravity is a harsh mistress. The birth of water has no witnesses. Her kitchen adagios suggest alchemy. A mature tomato contains truth. Perhaps because red is everyone's secret.

41

Fragility is apparent in her wrists, where pliancy delves into translucent blue. The way the sideboards tremble. We sleep with arms heavy as wood. Breath, the small curls of apostrophes and arched commas leaving his lips. A mountain is synonymous with companionship. The book of the unspeakable sky is always open. Certain scents pervade thought. Rain becoming breezy. The art of augury taught by birds.

42

How can it be she levitated from the mountaintop? Firefly pose. Calendula seed resembles prehistoric skeletons, or the curled bodies of seahorses. Ask the ocean what it has seen. Infrared signatures of phosphorous. Searchlights canceling starlight. The sidereal hoverings of undiscovered birds. Her universe is now a larger place. Why should magnolia petals fall face down, hiding their beauty?

43

A retching cat is of many minds. Why does the tail precede the comet? A smudge in the sky. Saturn's rings are made of ice. A number waits in a field which turns orange at the touch. A room was made of trials. Whereupon a countryside keeps for a week. Did lemons grow in the new world? This is dictation from stars.

44

My mind is made of water, and everything divides into fluidity. This island of wherefore, an alibi framed by charm. A secret device by which hindsight happens. You are a falling form of sleet. The skins of lizards abide on the bodies of lizards. I must banish vanity. They too experienced the day of their creation at some point in time. Scavengers lacking little in coat. The reptilian heart is made of time.

45

Having once lived in a tantrum. If ever I walked upon a landscape of twinkling lights. She became meeker than a thin line. A lowly role in the pack. Once I wouldn't have followed another. Fear of venture, what rope trick finds me here? He stood near the church gate, in a garbage bag, leaves in his hair. I went everyday to the orchards, sending regards. Writing those thank you's upon a particular ledge.

Remember the dead with a gift of gypsum. A pipe shall be a binding instrument. He didn't finish building the coffin, but instead stepped into a lake. We are nearly, all of us sailboats. Offer the four winds sackcloth remains. The seeds of ferns are invisible. Likewise, the possessor of fern seed is invisible. A drop of blood buried under a rosebush assures a ruddy complexion. Willow was worn by a discarded lover.

A seal swims in pink waters. The red tree is certain to find me. His helpless destinations became nowhere in mind, where luck pronounces soil. Forbidden scent of floating gardens. Floralia. Sabrina's early haunt on the bosom of waters. Garlands put to sea. His hands became extensions of the landscapes he created, hovering forms. An island once underwater now awaits the return of trees.

Ravenstone renders its possessor invisible. Solomon's seal is balm of the warrior's wound. Upon two spoons she traveled. Strewings were prevalent. Everyday, an offering of one-hundred thousand blossoms. Chrysis set a torch near garlands and fell to sleep. Influence by caprice. Rush-rings and myrtle-berry chains. Laurel slips.

49

The morning becomes transparent, and blames uncertain weather. A wave of stillness broke along her clavicles. A cascade of glass robes. The complete range of motion describes a wide cone. Is the shoulder blade then a wing? She awoke upon a bank uncommon, unsought, not purely existing in that it was not yet believed. A winter eye finds privacy among the dross of white rushes. A pomegranate determines season. Brackish waters of the anecdotal sea.

50

The world as seen through a steady stream of honey.
Today I do not recognize my endeavors. They become
the morning gathering of moisture upon the cloak of a
lady's mantle. A calla lily. A broad green stalk with face
slightly hidden. If I say this again I'll ask the plants to
speak for me. And then I may learn to make soil. This
coming and going ashore may rip me to shreds. Sight is
the least reliable of the senses.

51

A sketch of a young girl done in pastels, leaning against a fence. One complete summer is in her hand. Small slips of paper make everything happen. The edges are easiest to imagine, brown and unhindered. She didn't have a dance card. She would have to remember where the signature had been placed, dangling from the wrist of the calla lily. She is now caught up with her portrait. When they stop dancing, the world ends. She hadn't mastered the memory until she had held it for one complete reason.

52

When it is summer in hindsight, but now it is spring. Return those messages first which matter most. Seed sounds. Placing messages upon a matter scale to determine an order. Flounders make checkerboards with their bodies. I cut the fish out of water, a paper stenciled seafan. Is this the voice of the radio? It could have been the sound of streetlamps, water over dishes, or the sound of their feet muffled as they walked secretly at night. This sketch of a young girl I hardly know.

53

Traveling is treacherous since the order and meaning of endeavor is recast. I return to find that I have misplaced myself. The tree outside has switched sides, and its lattices have grown. The floor is staid and will no longer speak. I walk directly across from one previous life to another, and both are in relief, so that we may tell the tissue paper clouds apart from the tissue paper mountains. A face is impressed within this looking glass. And it is not my own. An entire vocabulary consisting of one concentrated gaze. This map I am placing upon the wall represents the sunlight which falls beyond a calendar.

She dissolves, and resides momentarily within the tides of a lungless fish. Pasts once inhabited, are no longer viable dwellings, and yet they still have the ability to beckon with sonorous voices, spun upon water. To lose, one must first possess. A storm was traveling towards those who sought protection in walls. The pulse beyond windows is memorial, a caustic framing; stone observatories overlook gardens. Purchased points of reference: a coin of ocean, the rents of corroboration. If there is nowhere to be, there is no hour. Petals elapse shape. Who subtitles her name?

55

Breath may be employed to seek a wandering apparition, by rowing towards the edge of a bank of shadow. From within the season of veils, ice crystals, once buried in the earth escape to mingle with the air until I am ensconced within a cloud of draughts. Potions which encourage the swimmer's stroke of luck, away from the entanglements of the past are illusory. Bodies of water are ambient dwellings. They suit the mind perfectly which is inhabited by phantoms. A place in my memory is reserved for you. Please send mementos. No spiral forecloses the past to one who has walked its many turns. And no past will speak, if you are not speaking kindly.

56

The morning is filled with invitations. My second destiny beckons. A sea of stars spread upon an expanse of shoulders. It must be near the millennium since copper fields have changed perceptibly. The sun appears such a star, I must bow my head. Soon we will check the calendar for years gone by, and then we will plant pastures to cry upon. His hands were directly sewn. If I tilt my head at odd angles then objects appear which did not exist before. A flower of forgetfulness adorns a pillow.

Venus is the looking-glass star. I do not explain the sensation of being newly divided. Cleft from and upon oneself, and blended with the bedrock of another. It is as indescribable as birth. The room had no door, only a window which painted the bedclothes. We stayed here as long as we dared, among the wax drippings. Desire riveting, the fragile revolver rose. Opposites reverse so temperature is wavelike. Where the night air was changed to heavy shawls, and the ocean clung to our heels.

58

The sky contains rain which is not pouring forth. Limit of ecstasies. We placed the fermentation locks upon the dandelion wine, and then went to sleep for three months. A mosaic drenched. I am watering my house. A watchband marks my place. The horse-chestnut trees are flowering. It is the fifth season of hovering. They confused themselves with their habits, and so became habitual.

59

I recall the music of the brittle stars, describing figure eights in their movements. As we fell down upon the hillside, the fragrance pressed against our bones. Saint Gabriel bristled with pardoned fire. His dusk covered body. An early awning of gold. Sounds uttered in my ears, *heavy snow*, or *heavy silence*. The madrona tree which speaks to the night. He recognized the labyrinth of the ear. This proves the corporeality of air.

60

The rose resin clung to my hands, as did the countryside.
Small dark lines moving over the blossoms are aphids.
They reproduce before they are born. I wished for the
ability to wander the landscape with no sense of division.
The separation of matter by thought, is a fleeting mis-
conception. As the shadows of how many birds have
crossed over me. A blink of shade. Like the orange hon-
eysuckle, Lonicera ciliosa, called "ghost" or "owl's
swing." The leaf surrounds the flower, and then cleaves.

61

The ice crystals in the plane window reached as high as the line of clouds visible. Given speed, all things disappear. She searched for the propeller, a blur of movement. It appeared from nowhere, among the scotch broom and beachgrass. The realms which I have been visiting of late are not accountable for their mutable edges. I am unable to articulate my coordinates. Everything of consequence today consisted of discourse. A fluid horse walks only on water. A tepid lake is the sky's reply.

62

Light rain amidst sunlight is a good luck omen. I should have subscribed to the season of storms. Everything mimics the foliage. I cannot speak as if I were not slipping from my chair. The sky is darkening now at four o'clock. Night descends a trumpet vine. I've lost my sleep in a drinking glass. The moods of celestial guardians cannot be tested upon ice or litmus. The hidden appeal of a nightmare is the ability to wake.

63

She had an admirable hand when writing letters, which cannot be replicated here. Some say she was seduced by poisonous thorns, and a dress made entirely of frowns. She cleans everything in her possession with a birch broom. Her name is of fraught iron, an emberless script. Sequel to a ship. Her candle carries itself, a late bronze bird. Her city, a cascade of fuel. A tidal theory of light. Dimensionless milk.

64

Is there a discrete frequency as we grow towards white hair, and ash clouds? Does ash ascend? Between where I sit, and six o'clock is an island where the bearded seal sits. The past is an empty platter. She was able to balance a raw egg on end, any day of the year. A damaged room is repaired by prayer. No landscape is shallow, and yet the charm of this countryside seems to be all in its coats. These are the necessities for the resuscitation of salt. Mimosas and contralto aside, within the pale of dross laws.

65

With leaf flutterings she may leave this land. This country of foxes and interpolations. The heroine who does not know her heart corresponds to the season of insurmountable eclipses. Perhaps her silences will be replaced with a type of flexible rope. The burden of thought could not be buried, so was carried to the centers of flowers where pollen caused drowsiness. A straw house was summoned. She searched for the town at the end of the road. Where there was no town to be found.

66

One who carries the diaphragm in a soundless case may understand why everything rings. The arc of each rib circling the lungs. Like a square neckline, a perfect frame. She wanted a compress for her heart. Something I should not harbor, like a ship or a gull. The melancholy implied by margins, the isolation of borders, the triviality of edgings. How to pull one body from two, and to call it a third, and not to be otherwise? I did not ask the faces around the fire, but those faces within the fire. There is nothing, no microscope which can find me as the season changes.

It seemed impossible that she could have such flying fingers, sleeveless bargain. Issuing forth seasons from the corner of her skirt. The function of night is an uncomplicated opera. The floors had vanished, and so we walked according to hermetic notations. Shall I spill these words before me, removing their husks and ambassadors? Things appeared differently from the other side of a glass. She concocted the garden from underneath the soil. A room into which light is never permitted to enter is required for making weather. The kohl trees embossed a brief reverie.

Standing among the remains of discarded skeletons had become unfashionable, so they walked about carrying their bones. Traces of the discarded sky could be carried easily in a large bucket and spilled against the edges of dawn. Harvested ice had been transformed into a system of nomenclature. Her complexion reveals the toil of such days. She eats again what she has spat out. Sparse word envelopes. Tired of youth, he summoned his further lives. The cat was begging for cream. This completes my library of books and bookish rogues.

69

The coming solstice sleeps within nothingness, so that the mind runs fluidly in no given direction. Her own lashes sundered her eye. A location where one might not be found is a traveling-chest of medicines. The most intricate existence may carry no mouthpiece. Finger holes wane as the most delicate wreathe contracts. The gold flute of an eavesdropper quivers as the sharp axe. Hands of sorrow are tied to the wishless. Chanting may replace begging. The June sun winters, uncommon as wrinkled glass.

Rain dropping off the eaves of a house makes parts of speech bow their heads. Looking out through a window I saw the fronds of summer encamped. Maimed sorrowing railroads. His book of sealife contains the downward stroke. Fiddler crabs pale in the evenings. She burrows backward using her more posterior legs. The floor and walls rock. Keys are not needed for leaving days that a door does not measure.

71

She lives upon sand dollars. A third decade was passed, rowing upon Turn Island. The wind became an anchor. Fields of copper began crimsoning. The light had taken a longer path home. Crepuscular foxes swam upon a river of red grass. Islands appeared in the night sky. Unaccountable rafts appeared to summon passengers. A cane wept, and a mattress succumbed to bury matches in its center.

72

A literate girlhood is a protective envelope. Diarists'
tracks were noted across yards of georgette. The few
lines allotted each day are the daughter cells of a steeple,
or as some would have it, a snuff box of morbid charms.
Some lenses are shaped for posterity. Others breed point-
lace. Shipboard diseases imprint havoc on the clearness
to a calling. From brothel to high mass within an hour.
Errands into wilderness. I made my way homeward with
a basket of yarrow

Coatlike in a swallow's nest, I fed my doves. Unlike the principle of blood revenge, red tides are not always red. Virtuous dreams may contain a montage of tempests. My eyes swell with trivial lurchings, no doubt the drama of the countryside causes one to fill a glass with many potions. The mating rituals of the goat cannot be called courting. Kindred rootlets form an anchor. He lives in a house of eaves. Night is often associated with molting. The inferno of summer glossed over, leaving them dressed in ferns.

74

The red center of a sea-angel is an embroidered lockable diary. Her new limb unfolds from a sac. A sheep is never shorn on the head. Conjugated shrimp: shrimped, shrumpingforth, shrimpering. The wood louse is often depressed. They live buried in mud. Vampire squid are kept in jewel boxes. Limb loss is a common event in the lives of many crustaceans. There are no flying snails.

This counterfeit novella I carry wistfully to the gallows. In passing, the eye of a peacock. As if wolves were verdant, or shepherds. As if the meridians of a piano were marked with talc. Locusts gather as I read, unfettered within coves of slate. The day passes iridescent, dangling as a fetish from the helm of a palpable ferry. I swore an oath upon handkerchiefs, that the smallest gesture may own the deepest initiative. The oath was marked by a procession of candlesticks. I was desired to eat, but as I had no stomach, I secretly stowed milk and tapioca in a barrel.

Mattresses filled with pine needles are a sleeping tonic. The mountains turned to my thoughts. I can make no other words out of June. I carried an heirloom of laurel brethren. A woeful lung. An ocular shovel. A crowd of numerologists gathered to count the loamy marsh ledgers, strolling forward with scrupulous tinkering. Pink witnesses were overlooking the tableau with transparent funnels. An inborn captive was tied at every waist, worn blunt as a culling nickel.

Let me lay into this belief; wind shook the three corners of the sail. She coveted red. The yellow flowers bled, covered with gold scarabs. Had I recorded every bit of her speech it would have been so. A photograph of sincere wanderings. Three hearts were pressed together as she bowed her head. A caravan of clouds was traveling by roads. I broached the weather-eye. These are all of my notes upon silence.

A bird carries my mind in a nest. Thoughts may cement themselves to brows. Who can knowingly recommend daylight to the evening primrose? Thirst is an accomplice. I tell this one leaf at a time. She was clipped and carried ashore. I bring no ribbon, as nothing belongs to me. She is assuming those years which I have not yet come upon. The change from fresh to sea waters.

I wished for the devices of the squid. A steady pen in place of a skeleton, and the ability to shroud myself with ink. Those oceanic correspondences cannot be lately regrettable as they leave no permanent markings. If water were my medium, I should not consider paper steady. Limp ledgers, and nebulous washes. The first letter appeared in the Cambrian period, at a depth of six hundred meters. The reply, an elaborate display of color. A walk above this streaming wake. Thus I may find my voice in the middle of a boatride, and carry it back with me between teeth and tongue.

80

I consoled myself with sand cameos. Within the shoulder of the allergy pageant, anything could send me into spasms. I lost my sheep, every means by which to measure myself. He dug through the mudflats, searching for ambergris. Figureheads live upon custom. By tracks they locate the sea-hare. By mouth they monitor tides. A blunt stove was filled with poplars. Moored upon an island which could not have existed, unless those perverse nursery books proved true.

81

She has been permitted outside of time in order to unclasp the frequency of night. Laurel oath, a barren chamber. Why was I not permitted to remain alone when no one accompanied me to the cottage? The "balm of sisterly consolation" may harness hedge and ditch. A sheep is an island in a sea of grass and a bird stands upon his back. While knowing the hand whose glance is fastened upon her still, her memory glass is sealed with wax. I've made opal pools for her hands. A kerchief of paper poppies. I lit a candle upon the wake, and resigned myself to wait.

Tying all sails to themselves, I requested my true bearings. Does radial symmetry suggest that the right and left hemispheres of the heart are mirror images? Solitary forms are connected by simple outfoldings of the body wall. We spotted the fox with the fox-viewing barnacles. Rodlike colonies set to reefbuilding. Gulls inspired the wind. The sky was perpetually lifted. Such simple bones. The last variable ash traced imperceptibly.

Goat's beard hung above in bunches, as lanterns at dusk. Wind made charcoal etchings and thumbprints, moving in circular patterns on the lagoon. Emerging from the dark woods the ground had paled to gray-white dust. One angle of sky scalded pink, underscored by mottled clouds. A newly hatched moth, drying its brightly colored wings. We heard the music of the organ pipe coral. Red meadows turned redder. Until the entire field had gone aflame. I did not engrave these surface edges, but came upon them once in a corridor and have kept the replica ever since.

84

A male spider will court the severed leg of a female, or the evaporated washings of her body. He might pluck a familiar music upon her web. Luminescence is intrinsic. The sea pen shimmers when touched. The squid only darkens when disturbed. An octopus in distress may display his colors. A striped hue pattern establishes a temporary bond between cuttlefish. Scorpion courtship consists of promenading. They are secretive, but can be seen at night clearly with an ultraviolet light.

85

Even in families which build webs to catch prey, eventually all blood vessels unite with the heart. She cast off her arms, congenial as midnight. Garments hewn of a former lifetime. She carried a silken egg case. Attached her dragline to the crossbridges. Her pearl-white eyes were once mistaken for eclipses. She locks her spine in place. Her poison gland pitchpoling as she turns. Her nightbook— a trapdoor which plummets into a small pouch of leaves.

The starfish is neither star, nor fish. The town was one vacuous bedroom. She was born unobtrusively, upon a staunch rock. Leveling with the eye, this horizon was mended as she fell. Avoiding treasonous invitations is one method of avoiding a stroll along a brief plank. The limestone walls of her heart were careless of pitch, and could not be summoned. Only their formations, caves and stalagmites changed by the slow dripping of water. Where the discarded spots of fawns reside, is colorless blood. She follows a damsel fly to dead man's cove.

So the petticoat was in the beginning, furrowed, mangled, ghastly. The first flag was made of a sailor's blue coat moved to strange symphonies. All of this I learned while in the apple barrel. He spoke of my ghost maneuverings, as if I had been two places at once. I did not answer the accusation, but remained near the mast. My brooding basket, and bower covered with flagstones. My dungeon is coved and vaulted. The many-eyed scallops became scavenging deckhands. Ballooning spiders covered the sails, carried through air currents by means of silken thread.

88

I lay awake, awaiting the true spring. I kept the auspicious pages near my bedside. The incomplete waking of cicadas. The boulevard of June, up the night filled street raised and lowered like a hem. These words were stolen from silence. Each encased in an intricate body. There is such non-believing sleep. Only the right hand knows how to open doors. Only the right eye sees distances.

The sky, a breech of color, sends a slight gray edging above the pointed line of trees. The present occurs here, without consent. The hours pass as if on paper. Mary had a little mayhem. Moving effortlessly through the thin medium of air. Jars of oil become redder; flowers bleed upon the death of a saint. Candles teal in silver holders, the yellow centers visible when lit. Lorelie held a little lamprey. A little lamprey also provides light.

Why supposing a balance is more difficult with eyes closed. In sympathy with rooms, objects, in sympathy with messengers. Locket consoling which way is exactitude. I engraved upon a piece of driftwood, but the words were taken back by water. This happened on a day sullen. Covered with rain. As an eye covered with mist may miss a whetstone. Recourse is unrecordable. Concave letters think.

91

She had written her hopes upon all kinds of scaffoldings. I wished, and the mill was at my side. The plot of this shore will be a type of horizon. A book dreams nothing. It is the waterline. The dreams exactly. I have mended my threshold and come alongside dreaming. The surface of the cell is quiescent. Hands remain fragments of the day.

The coming storm tarnishes silver. The letter began inside her hand. *I must protect myself somehow.* The message was returned, "I am not she." The golden pears tempt me; blushing permits a pressing forth. When I turn on the light, I cease to exist. Streetlights are appropriating this time of falling night, as the span of a day quickens, and within one interior a body of water sleeps with no tiredness, no reservation. My ties to this world have been bound by an invisible hand, less likely my own. I cannot imagine her average of tears.

93

Mark all sentences that do not seem to belong "else-where" and then find a place for them. The obligatory shoe scurries, multiplying. Yet "the place of elsewhere" may not exist. Perhaps instead of "mark" she had written "marl." I recognize the face of this postcard well, swathed in taffeta, tea-length scorn. To "marl" seemed an inevitable crux, a hovering sphere of elsewhere which was knotted and scarred. Ultimately hidden. "I", a hidden intention, slipped in a momentary fog. The landscape may pretend nothing, and I everything.

94

That we exist only within pictures must not be insisted upon. The photographs were silvering upon themselves, drowning into dimensions which could not be spoken of. Having no clock, I must rely upon historical forecasts. Once inside the corn-pollen-blessing, I find another path sprinkled before me. A procession of tiny suns, following crevices into the earth. The point is very much like walking without looking back upon one's heels. As the thief who compressed my living quarters to a sigh. Leaving me with no sail but a harp, little sleep, and hardly any anchor. Or perhaps I had sent away a bird, but the bird traveled back to greet me.

To my concealed mapmaker: I can only say that I had no idea of the gravity of these events before setting forth within them, as if to sail a ship while looking at a picture. Then the house will begin to wake. The mist lifts, unmarked upon spirit. Where a word of roads ends has considered walking. Perhaps we are buried. One night in the day of the forest. Choruses of fire will be performing in St. Mark's Cathedral. An oak tree planted over one's ashes imprisons the spirit. As does the wax rose.

She ran off with a pair of initials. Taking flight from the hand. Her charcoal collars are lifted, and she carries a bouquet of fever trees. To explain this portrait one could summon the slow youth of her planet. The type is smaller than I remember, and the spines of sleeping carriages cast shadows with which to keep warm. A seance at large follows the dead. Despite aerial views, she sees no larks. The way a birdcage in a basement does not suggest birds, or contain sunlight. A counterweight for walking in the woods.

The day is too cold for such a garden party as planned. My blood I fear, would congeal. I looked for her name under pneumonia. This being said, motives may be elliptical. At the velvet hour, episodes during which red plumes of sea ice form a terraced inlet. The ice caves threw off sheets of cold air. Which concealed us. A hopeful rag of moments, was spurned and thrown blamefully to the fire. The night had hidden within her simple palm.

Wandering through a dark house, water is a constant escort to the weight of the head. An eye is willing to walk through prior worlds of charmed calyxes, estates of whim, summer psalteries, smeared upon the white neck of a goose. Where the goose goes, go her words, her meaningful drawbacks. Without any such smudge involved to objectify the night, whose body became a decoration and embellishment upon every one of her thoughts. She was given no memento, no dusk, and no threshold, but entrusts her entire faith to the lace upon a slip of night, white between the violet silhouette of leaves, the meandering footsteps of a lake. An intrusion of illogical prose, clawing her lip in reverie. A locket closed and opened, within syllables of sea-length. Beside a necklace of words, limbic emotions shared with birds. The wishbone, a profile in sway.

In sleep the myriad hands. In sleep is a parade of most familiar weather. My attempts at recordkeeping, bird-tracks, trails of tiny feet. Upon the floor of the dream written in palimpsest, an equinoctial figure reads each letter as an article of cloth, peruses the stitching, and disrobes. I traveled until all water had been removed from me, until the ocean turned away, and tied tourniquets upon her wrists. This sea-drenched cloth pulled about the waist, and over the head. This dream transcribed and sent had become true, before the second dreamer woke. To lie "in wait," between air and sea, is also a summons towards the unknown. "Larvae," the ghost imprint before birth, whose hand held those fingers I claimed as my own.

Laynie Browne is the author of four previous collections of poetry, most recently, *Drawing of a Swan Before Memory*, Winner of the Contemporary Poetry Series (University of Georgia Press, 2005), *Pollen Memory* (Tender Buttons, 2003) and *Acts of Levitation*, a novel (Spuyten Duyvil, 2003). Recent chapbooks include *Webs of Argiope* (Phylum Press 2005) and a collaboration with Lee Ann Brown titled *Nascent Toolbox* (The Owl Press 2004). She is former co-curator of The Subtext Reading Series in Seattle, and The Ear Inn in NYC. She has taught poetry-in-the-schools as a visiting artist in New York City, and Seattle, and has taught creative writing at University of Washington-Bothell, and Mills College. She currently lives in Oakland, California.

SPUYTEN DUYVIL

1881471772	**6/2/95**	DONALD BRECKENRIDGE
193313223X	**8TH AVENUE**	STEFAN BRECHT
1881471942	**ACTS OF LEVITATION**	LAYNIE BROWNE
1933132221	**ALIEN MATTER**	REGINA DERIEVA
1881471748	**ANARCHY**	MARK SCROGGINS
1881471675	**ANGELUS BELL**	EDWARD FOSTER
188147142X	**ANSWERABLE TO NONE**	EDWARD FOSTER
1881471950	**APO/CALYPSO**	GORDON OSING
1933132248	**APPLES OF THE EARTH**	DINA ELENBOGEN
1881471799	**ARC: CLEAVAGE OF GHOSTS**	NOAM MOR
1881471667	**ARE NOT OUR LOWING HEIFERS SLEEKER THAN NIGHT-SWOLLEN MUSHROOM**	
		NADA GORDON
0972066276	**BALKAN ROULETTE**	DRAZAN GUNJACA
1881471241	**BANKS OF HUNGER AND HARDSHIP**	J. HUNTER PATTERSON
1881471624	**BLACK LACE**	BARBARA HENNING
1881471918	**BREATHING FREE**	VYT BAKAITIS (ED.)
1881471225	**BY THE TIME YOU FINISH THIS BOOK YOU MIGHT BE DEAD**	
		AARON ZIMMERMAN
1881471829	**COLUMNS: TRACK 2**	NORMAN FINKELSTEIN
0972066284	**CONVICTION & SUBSEQUENT LIFE OF SAVIOR NECK**	
		CHRISTIAN TEBORDO
1881471934	**CONVICTIONS NET OF BRANCHES**	MICHAEL HELLER
1881471195	**CORYBANTES**	TOD THILLEMAN
1881471306	**CUNNING**	LAURA MORIARTY
1881471217	**DANCING WITH A TIGER**	ROBERT FRIEND
1881471284	**DAY BOOK OF A VIRTUAL POET**	ROBERT CREELEY
1881471330	**DESIRE NOTEBOOKS**	JOHN HIGH
1881471683	**DETECTIVE SENTENCES**	BARBARA HENNING
1881471357	**DIFFIDENCE**	JEAN HARRIS
1881471802	**DONT KILL ANYONE, I LOVE YOU**	GOJMIR POLAJNAR
1881471985	**EVIL QUEEN**	BENJAMIN PEREZ
1881471837	**FAIRY FLAG AND OTHER STORIES**	JIM SAVIO
1881471969	**FARCE**	CARMEN FIRAN
188147187X	**FLAME CHARTS**	PAUL OPPENHEIMER
1881471268	**FLICKER AT THE EDGE OF THINGS**	LEONARD SCHWARTZ
1933132027	**FORM**	MARTIN NAKELL
1881471756	**GENTLEMEN IN TURBANS, LADIES CAULS**	JOHN GALLAHER
1933132132	**GESTURE THROUGH TIME**	ELIZABETH BLOCK
1933132078	**GOD'S WHISPER**	DENNIS BARONE
1933132000	**GOWANUS CANAL, HANS KNUDSEN**	TOD THILLEMAN
1881471586	**IDENTITY**	BASIL KING
1881471810	**IN IT WHATS IN IT**	DAVID BARATIER
0972066233	**INCRETION**	BRIAN STRANG
0972066217	**JACKPOT**	TSIPI KELLER
1881471721	**JAZZER & THE LOITERING LADY**	GORDON OSING
1881471926	**KNOWLEDGE**	MICHAEL HELLER
193313206X	**LAST SUPPER OF THE SENSES**	DEAN KOSTOS
1881471470	**LITTLE TALES OF FAMILY AND WAR**	MARTHA KING

0972066241	**LONG FALL**	ANDREY GRITSMAN
0972066225	**LYRICAL INTERFERENCE**	NORMAN FINKELSTEIN
1933132094	**MALCOLM AND JACK**	TED PELTON
1933132086	**MERMAID'S PURSE**	LAYNIE BROWNE
1881471594	**MIOTTE**	RUHRBERG & YAU (EDS.)
097206625X	**MOBILITY LOUNGE**	DAVID LINCOLN
1881471322	**MOUTH OF SHADOWS**	CHARLES BORKHUIS
1881471896	**MOVING STILL**	LEONARD BRINK
1881471209	**MS**	MICHAEL MAGEE
1881471853	**NOTES OF A NUDE MODEL**	HARRIET SOHMERS ZWERLING
1881471527	**OPEN VAULT**	STEPHEN SARTARELLI
1933132116	**OSIRIS WITH A TROMBONE ACROSS THE SEAM OF INSUBSTANCE**	
		JULIAN SEMILIAN
1881471977	**OUR DOGS**	SUSAN RING
1881471152	**OUR FATHER**	MICHAEL STEPHENS
0972066209	**OVER THE LIFELINE**	ADRIAN SANGEORZAN
1933132256	**PIGS DRINK FROM INFINITY**	MARK SPITZER
1881471691	**POET**	BASIL KING
0972066292	**POLITICAL ECOSYSTEMS**	J.P. HARPIGNIES
1933132051	**POWERS: TRACK 3**	NORMAN FINKELSTEIN
1933132191	**RE-TELLING**	TSIPI KELLER
1881471454	**RUNAWAY WOODS**	STEPHEN SARTARELLI
1933132035	**SAIGON & OTHER POEMS**	JACK WALTERS
1933132167	**SARDINE ON VACATION**	ROBERT CASTLE
1881471888	**SEE WHAT YOU THINK**	DAVID ROSENBERG
1933132124	**SHEETSTONE**	SUSAN BLANSHARD
1881471640	**SPIN CYCLE**	CHRIS STROFFOLINO
1881471578	**SPIRITLAND**	NAVA RENEK
1881471705	**SPY IN AMNESIA**	JULIAN SEMILIAN
1933132213	**STRANGE EVOLUTIONARY FLOWERS**	LIZBETH RYMLAND
188147156X	**SUDDENLY TODAY WE CAN DREAM**	RUTHA ROSEN
1933132175	**SUNRISE IN ARMAGEDDON**	WILL ALEXANDER
1881471780	**TEDS FAVORITE SKIRT**	LEWIS WARSH
1933132043	**THINGS THAT NEVER HAPPENED**	GORDON OSING
1933132205	**THIS GUY**	JAMES LEWELLING
1933132019	**THREE MOUTHS**	TOD THILLEMAN
1881471365	**TRACK**	NORMAN FINKELSTEIN
188147190X	**TRANSGENDER ORGAN GRINDER**	JULIAN SEMILIAN
1881471861	**TRANSITORY**	JANE AUGUSTINE
1933132140	**VIENNA ØØ**	EUGENE K. GARBER
1881471543	**WARP SPASM**	BASIL KING
188147173X	**WATCHFULNESS**	PETER O'LEARY
1881471993	**XL POEMS**	JULIUS KELERAS
0972066268	**YOU, ME, AND THE INSECTS**	BARBARA HENNING

All Spuyten Duyvil titles are available through your local bookseller via
Booksense.com

Distributed to the trade by Biblio Distribution (a division of NBN)
1-800-462-6420   *bibliodistribution.com*